Kids' Travel Guide
Italy & Rome

FlyingKids Presents:

Kids' Travel Guide

Italy & Rome

Authors: Elisa Davoglio & Shiela H. Leon

Editor: Carma Graber

Graphic Designer: Neboysha Dolovacki

Cover Illustrations and design: Francesca Guido

Visit us @ www.theflyingkids.com

Contact us: leonardo@theflyingkids.com

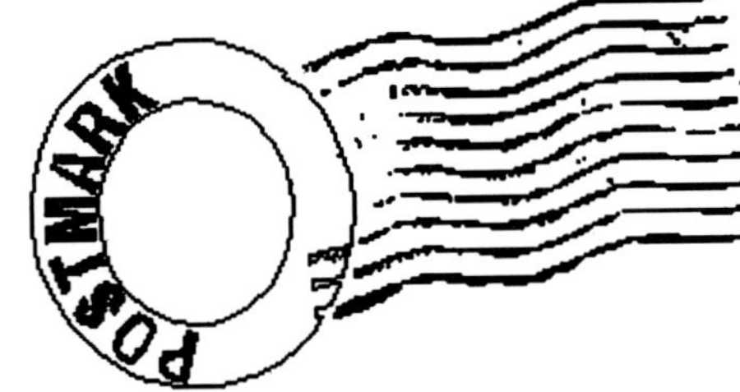

ISBN: 978-1499677843

Acknowledgement:

All images are from Diomedia or public domain except those mentioned below:

Dreamstime: 41m; Canstockphoto: 13m, 48mc; Dollar Photo Club: 17m, 24mb, 44mbcl, 44mbcr, 44mr, 45bg; Shutterstock: 49mt, 49mc, 49mb, 50mt, 52mb, 55mc, 55mb, 63mb.

Attributions: 19m-By Roberto Vicario (Roberto Vicario) [CC BY-SA 3.0 (http://creativecommons.org/licenses/by-sa/3.0)], via Wikimedia Commons; 32bg to 42bg-© Tripomatic, 2014. Built using data from Tripomatic, CloudMade and OpenStreetMap.org contributors; 50mb-RomaForoRomanoMiliariumAureum" by MM; 52mb-By Jaakko Luttinen (Own work) [CC BY-SA 3.0 (http://creativecommons.org/licenses/by-sa/3.0)], via Wikimedia Commons.

Key: t=top; b=bottom; l=left; r=right; c=center; m=main image; bg=background

Table of Contents

This is the only page for parents in this book ...

Dear parents,

If you bought this book, you're probably planning a family trip with your kids. You are spending a lot of time and money in the hopes that this family vacation will be pleasant and fun. You would like your children to learn a little about the country you visit — its geography, history, unique culture, traditions, and more. And you hope they will always remember the trip as a very special experience.

The reality is often quite different. Parents find themselves frustrated as they struggle to convince their kids to join a tour or visit a landmark, while the kids just want to stay in and watch TV. On the road, the children are glued to their mobile devices instead of enjoying the new sights. Many parents are disappointed after they return home and discover that their kids don't remember much about the trip and the new things they learned.

That's exactly why *Kids' Travel Guide — Italy & Rome* was created. With *Kids' Travel Guide — Italy & Rome*, young children become researchers and active participants in the trip. They learn fun facts about history and culture; they play games and take quizzes. This helps kids — and parents — enjoy the trip a lot more!

How does it work?

A family trip is fun. But difficulties can arise when children are not in their natural environment. *Kids' Travel Guide — Italy & Rome* takes this into account and supports children as they get ready for the trip, visit new places, learn new things, and finally, return home. The *Kids' Travel Guide — Italy & Rome* does this by helping children to prepare for the trip and know what to expect. During the trip, kids will read relevant facts about Italy and the city of Rome, and get advice on how to adapt to new situations. *Kids' Travel Guide — Italy & Rome* includes puzzles, tasks to complete, useful tips, and other recommendations along the way. All of this encourages children to experiment, explore, and be more involved in the family's activities — as well as to learn new information and make memories throughout the trip. In addition, kids are asked to document and write about their experiences during the trip, so that when you return home, they will have a memoir that will be fun to look at and reread again and again.

Kids' Travel Guide — Italy & Rome includes two parts: The first offers general information about Italy — basic geography; flags, symbols, and coins; basic history; and colorful facts about the country's culture and customs. The second part focuses on the city of Rome — its history and culture and all its interesting and unique attractions. It concentrates on central sites that are recommended for children. At each of these sites, interesting facts, action items, and quizzes await your kids. You, the parents, are invited to participate, or to find an available bench and relax while you enjoy your active children.

Ready for a new experience?

Have a nice trip and have fun!

Hi, Kids!

If you are reading this book, it means you are lucky — you are going to **Italy and Rome**!

You may have noticed that your parents are getting ready for the journey. They have bought travel guides, looked for information on the Internet, and printed pages of information. They are talking to friends and people who have already visited **Italy and Rome,** in order to learn about it and know what to do, where to go, and when … But this book is not just another guidebook for your parents.

This book is for you only — the young traveler.

First and foremost, meet Leonardo, your very own personal guide on this trip. Leonardo has visited many places around the world. (Guess how he got there?) He will be with you throughout the book and the trip. Leonardo will tell you all about the places you will visit — it is always good to learn a little bit about the city and country and their history beforehand. He will provide many ideas, quizzes, tips, and other surprises. Leonardo will accompany you while you are packing and leaving home. He will stay in the hotel with you (don't worry, it does not cost more money)! And he will see the sights with you until you return home.

Have Fun!

A travel diary — the beginning!

Going to Italy and Rome!!!

How did you get to Italy?

By plane / ship / car / other ____________

We will stay in Italy for ____________ days.

Is this your first visit ____________ ?

Where will you sleep? In a hotel / in a campsite / in a motel / in an apartment / with family / other ____________

What places are you planning to visit?

____

____

____

What special activities are you planning to do?

____

____

____

Are you excited about the trip?

This is an excitement indicator. Ask your family members how excited they are (from "not at all" up to "very, very much"), and mark each of their answers on the indicator. Leonardo has already marked the level of his excitement …

not at all — very, very much

Leonardo

Who is traveling?

Write down the names of the family members traveling with you and their answers to the questions.

Paste a picture of your family.

Name: ____________

Age: ________

Has he or she visited Italy and Rome before? yes / no

What is the most exciting thing about your upcoming trip?

____

____

____

Name: ____________

Age: ________

Has he or she visited Italy and Rome before? yes / no

What is the most exciting thing about your upcoming trip?

____

____

____

Name: ____________

Age: ________

Has he or she visited Italy and Rome before? yes / no

What is the most exciting thing about your upcoming trip?

____

____

____

Name: ____________

Age: ________

Has he or she visited Italy and Rome before? yes / no

What is the most exciting thing about your upcoming trip?

____

____

____

Name: ____________

Age: ________

Has he or she visited Italy and Rome before? yes / no

What is the most exciting thing about your upcoming trip?

____

____

____

Preparations at home — DO NOT FORGET ...!

Mom or Dad will take care of packing clothes (how many pairs of pants, which comb to take ...). Leonardo will only tell you the stuff he thinks you might want to take on your trip to Italy and Rome.

Here's the **Packing List** Leonardo made for you. You can check off each item as you pack it:

- ☐ *Kids' Travel Guide — Italy & Rome* — of course!
- ☐ Comfortable walking shoes
- ☐ A raincoat (One that folds up is best — sometimes it rains without warning ...)
- ☐ A hat (and sunglasses, if you want)
- ☐ Pens and pencils
- ☐ Crayons and markers (It is always nice to color and paint.)
- ☐ A notebook or a writing pad (You can use it for games or writing, or to draw or doodle in when you're bored ...)
- ☐ A book to read
- ☐ Your smartphone/tablet or camera
- ☐ ______________________
- ☐ ______________________

Welcome to Italy — the Beautiful Land

Italy is a magical place. Every year more than **40 million people** come to explore **Italy's many treasures**. It's one of the most popular countries to visit in the world — and you'll soon find out why!

In Italy, you can get an up-close look at fascinating **history** and famous **art** and **monuments**. You'll find exciting **cities**, beautiful **scenery**, wonderful **beaches, lots of delicious food** ... and more.

Italy's nickname is *Belpaese* — Italian for "beautiful land."

Leonardo can't wait to tell you all about this great country. Let's get started ...

Who knows which continent Italy is on? (Answer on the next page.)

Did you know?
Inside the country of Italy there are two independent nations: **Vatican City** and **the Republic of San Marino.**

The Republic of San Marino is one of the smallest countries in the world. It measures only **61 square km** (or **23½** square miles)!

Vatican City is located inside the city of Rome. It's the smallest country in the world: **0.44 square km** (or about 0.17 square miles). It is governed by the Pope, the head of the Catholic Church.

Did you know?
Italy has over 3,000 museums.

Italy on the map — can you see the BOOT?

Italy is easy to recognize on the map!

- It is located in western Europe.
- It's a peninsula — so it is bordered by the sea on three sides.

And Italy has the unusual shape of a boot!

A boot

Italy

TUNISIA

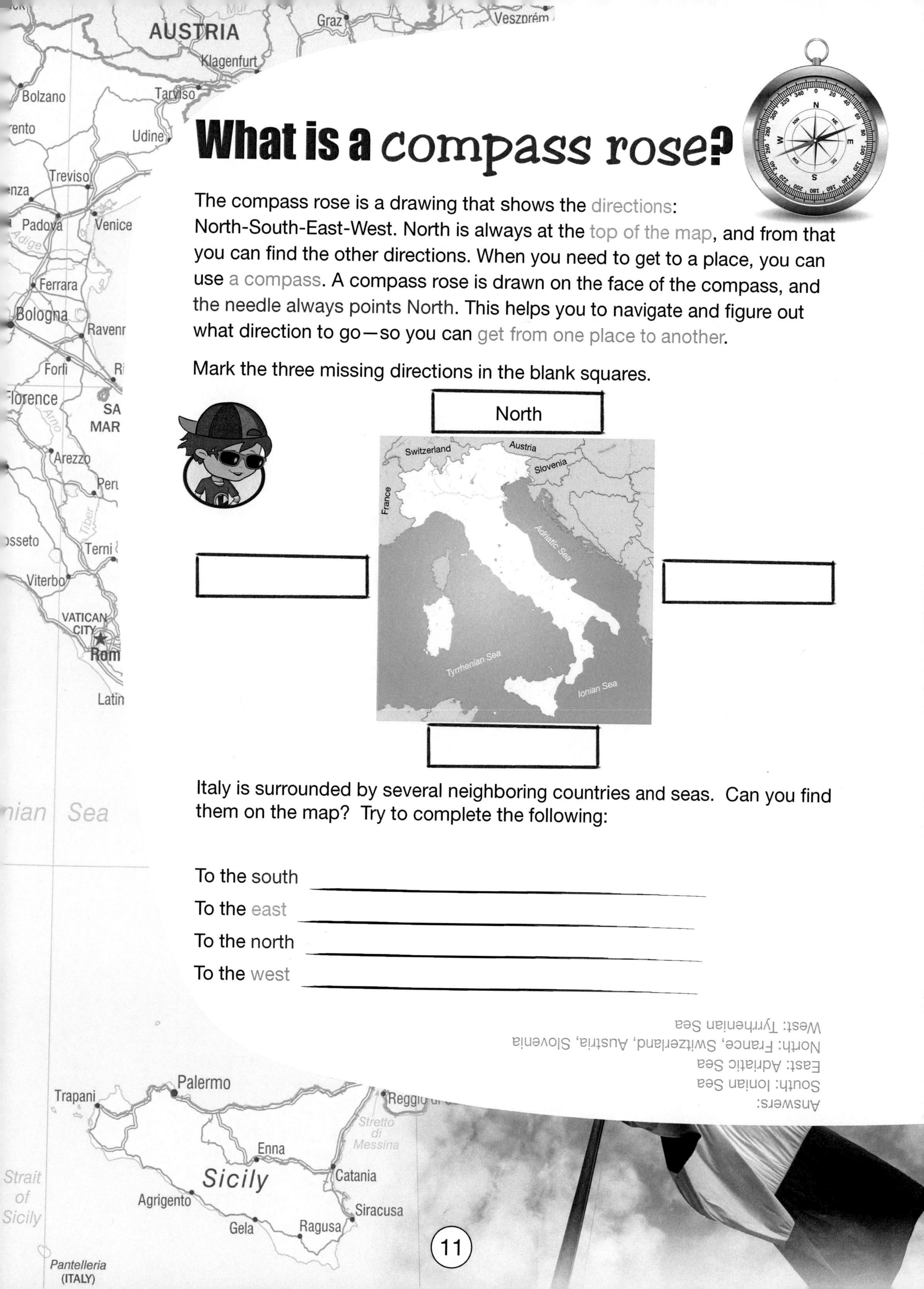

What is a compass rose?

The compass rose is a drawing that shows the directions: North-South-East-West. North is always at the top of the map, and from that you can find the other directions. When you need to get to a place, you can use a compass. A compass rose is drawn on the face of the compass, and the needle always points North. This helps you to navigate and figure out what direction to go—so you can get from one place to another.

Mark the three missing directions in the blank squares.

North

Italy is surrounded by several neighboring countries and seas. Can you find them on the map? Try to complete the following:

To the south ______________________

To the east ______________________

To the north ______________________

To the west ______________________

Answers:
South: Ionian Sea
East: Adriatic Sea
North: France, Switzerland, Austria, Slovenia
West: Tyrrhenian Sea

Italy's beautiful borders

Did you know? Borders were invented to separate different countries. A border is a line that marks the end of one country's territory and the beginning of another. There are all kinds of borders. Sometimes a river or a mountain range makes a natural border. And sometimes a fence or a special gate marks a border.

In Italy, there is a natural border to the north: the Italian Alps. These mountains separate Italy from the European countries of France, Switzerland, Austria, and Slovenia.

Italy is also bordered by the sea, and the country has two islands. What are they?

- Canary Islands
- Peter Pan Islands
- Sicily and Sardinia Islands

Answer: Sicily and Sardinia Islands

You are about to visit the beautiful cities of Italy. Can you find 10 cities in the word search puzzle?

✓ ROME
✓ FLORENCE
✓ VENICE
✓ PISA
✓ MILAN
✓ NAPLES
✓ PALERMO
✓ GENOVA
✓ PADOVA
✓ TORINO

R	A	O	I	E	N	C	E	A	M	F	G
E	O	R	D	S	G	Y	J	P	I	S	A
Q	E	M	U	S	K	Z	K	M	L	W	O
H	O	V	E	N	I	C	E	A	A	G	D
A	N	F	Z	F	L	O	R	E	N	C	E
C	A	M	X	L	O	R	I	N	Q	E	O
P	A	L	E	R	M	O	R	I	N	O	O
Y	D	S	G	I	R	K	Z	K	S	H	D
P	A	L	E	R	M	O	T	K	H	A	T
F	R	U	N	A	P	L	E	S	D	D	A
B	O	T	O	R	I	N	O	K	E	R	T
T	K	Z	V	A	N	S	I	E	S	Y	U
O	V	P	A	D	O	V	A	C	K	S	P

Major cities in Italy

Italy has some of the most famous cities in the world.
Fly around with Leonardo and learn about a few of them.

Florence — famous for art!

Florence is famous for being the city where many great Italian artists like **Leonardo da Vinci**, **Michelangelo**, **Giotto**, **Raphael**, and **Botticelli** were born and lived during the "**Renaissance**."*
Florence was actually the first city in all of Europe to have paved roads and streets!

*Renaissance is French for "rebirth." The Renaissance period started in Florence. There was a lot of new growth in the arts, architecture, and science.

Milan — the shopping capital!

Milan is the second largest city in Italy. It is Italy's shopping capital. It is famous worldwide for its fashion, and has some of the best shops in Europe.

Venice — the city of canals!

Venice sits in a lagoon on the Adriatic Sea. The city is made up of more than 100 tiny islands. No cars are allowed in the city! People get around by using the 400 footbridges and 170 boat canals. Gondolas are the most popular boats in Venice.

Naples — home of Mount Vesuvius!

Mount Vesuvius is one of three volcanos in Europe that is still active. But it hasn't erupted since 1944.
In ancient times, it erupted and caused a big earthquake that completely destroyed two cities: **Pompeii** and **Herculaneum**.

And of course ... Rome!

Rome is the capital of Italy — and there are so many fun things to see and do there! Leonardo can't wait to tell you all about it in the next part of this book ...

Flags, symbols, and coins

This is the tricolor (three-colored) flag of Italy. It's called *bandiera italiana* or *tricolore* in Italian.

Each color has a meaning:
Green stands for Hope and for the plains of Italy.
White stands for Faith and for the snow-capped Alps.
Red stands for Charity (love and kindness) and for the blood shed by those who fought for Italy's independence.

Did you know?
Italians are very proud of their flag. They respect and honor it as the most important symbol of their country. If you buy an Italian flag, remember that the flag should never be allowed to drag along the ground!

This emblem is the official symbol of Italy. It has a white star with a thin red border. The star's background is a cogwheel with five spokes. It's surrounded by two branches. Can you recognize what trees the branches represent?

Answer:
An olive tree and an oak tree

The Italian wolf is the animal symbol of Italy.

Get to know the COINS OF ITALY ...

Italy is part of the European Union. The country has replaced its own coins (*lira*) with euro coins since 2001. The Italian euro coins are easy to recognize because they show famous Italian art and places. Every coin has the letters "RI" for *Repubblica Italiana* (Italian Republic) and the letter "R" for Rome.

The most famous coin is worth one euro. This coin shows Leonardo da Vinci's drawing called *Vitruvian Man*.

Quizzes!

You want to buy a slice of pizza, and it costs 2.35 euros. How many coins will you have to use if you have only 5-cent euro coins?

Answer: 47 coins

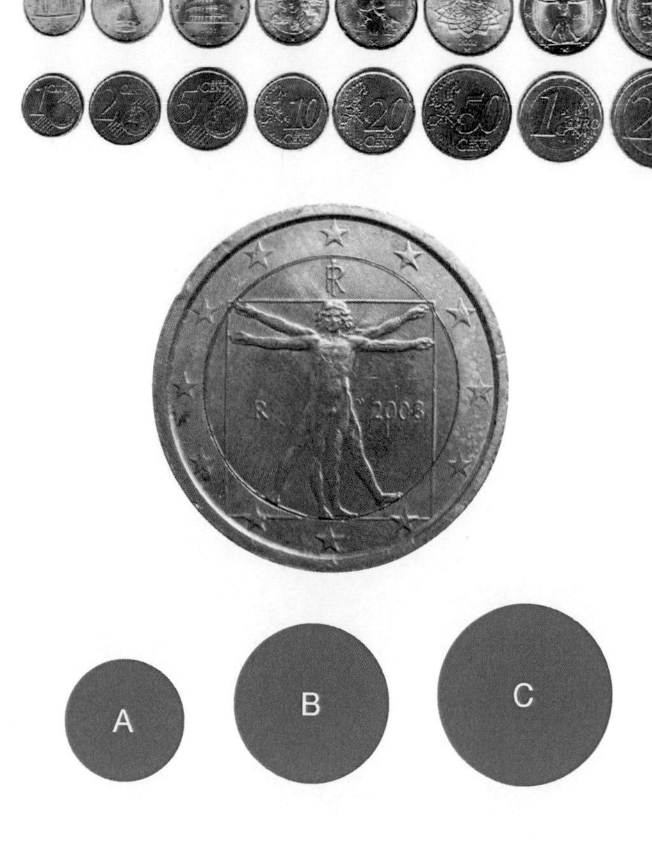

What Italian coins match the sizes below? Place coins on the circles and find the right answers!

Answers: A - 1 cent, B - 5 cent, C - 50 cent

Italy's LONG and SPECIAL history

Italy has a long history! Around 2,000 BC,* tribes of shepherds and farmers lived in little villages in Italy. These villages were often built on the banks of a river or in a fertile valley. Italy was very rich in natural resources, and its land was planted to grow everything necessary!

*BC stands for "before Christ," and AD means "after Christ." AD is short for the Latin phrase *anno Domini*. It means "in the year of the Lord's birth."

One of the small villages was **Rome**. According to a legend, twin brothers **Romulus and Remus** wanted to build a city, but they argued over where it should be. Romulus killed his brother and named the city after himself. Then he declared himself the first King of Rome.

The village of Rome was founded on the banks of the River Tiber in 753 BC. The village soon become a large town. It spread over the surrounding territory and all of Italy. During the next centuries, Rome grew into what is known as the **Roman Empire**.

The Roman Empire covered most of the known world in its time, as you can see on the map!

Compare the borders of Italy today with the Roman Empire! What modern countries would be part of Italy if it was still as big as the ancient Roman Empire?

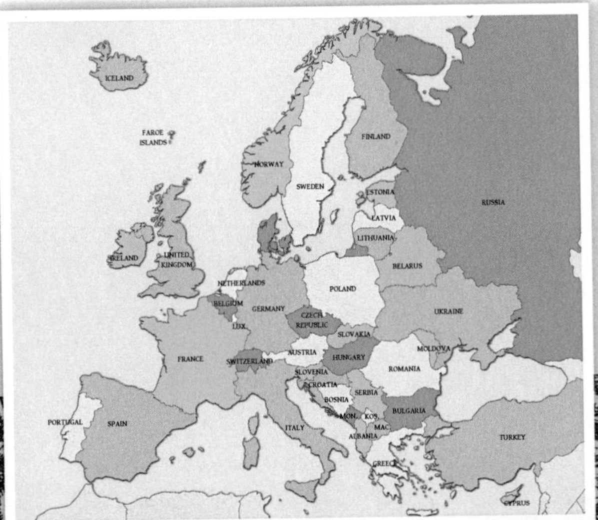

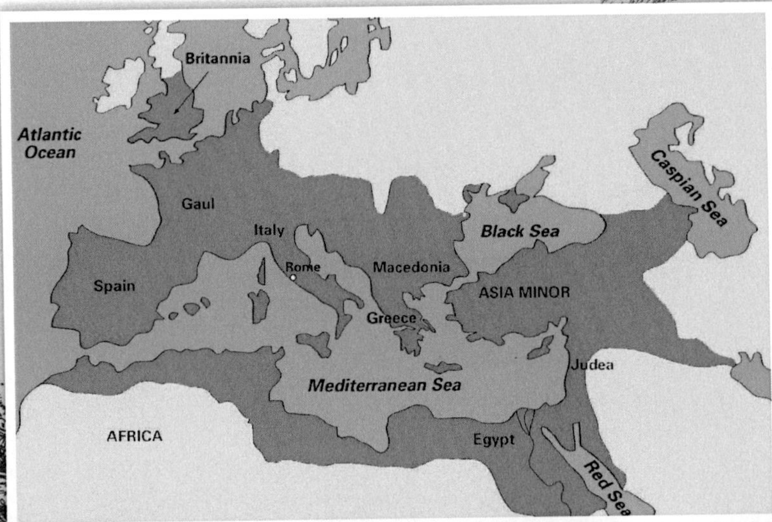

The mighty Roman Empire

Quizzes!

The Roman Empire covered

- 322 km (200 miles).
- 3.7 million km (2.3 million miles).
- The distance between the sun and the moon.

It had a population of

- 10,000 people.
- 5 billion people.
- 120 million people.

Answers:
3.7 million km (2.3 million miles);
120 million people

The Roman Empire was the biggest empire in the world for over four centuries. Its power extended everywhere. The Roman Empire ended in 493 AD. That's when Italy was invaded and conquered, and divided into many separate kingdoms.
The state of Rome was ruled by the Pope. The Popes were really like kings. They often entered battles to keep their land and their authority.

In 1861, Italy was officially re-united under a single king. And in 1870, the state of Rome was conquered and added to the kingdom of Italy.

Italy was a kingdom until 1946. Then after World War II, it became the republic it is today.

What's the difference between a kingdom and a republic?

A kingdom is a country ruled by a king or a queen. In a kingdom, the power passes to the king or queen's son or daughter, or to other members of the royal family. **A republic** is a country that is governed by representatives who are elected by the citizens.

We have talked a lot about Italy, now let's talk about the Italian people ...

ITALIANS and their culture

Italians are famous for being friendly and welcoming. They are very devoted to their families and friends. They like **being outdoors** to enjoy Italy's many **sunny days.**

Italians create lots of occasions to eat together, sing together, and play with children!

Playing football* is the most popular way to have fun with friends and parents! Even if you don't speak a word of Italian, it doesn't matter. If you are in a park or public garden, you'll always find someone to play football with you!

*Italian football is the game that is called soccer in North America.

Do you play football (soccer)? ____________

What is your favorite team? ____________

Do you know any famous Italian football players?

____

Did you know?

Most Italian people have the same habit. They talk with their hands as much as with their mouths. They use a lot of gestures. Sometimes you can tell what they're saying even if they don't speak English!

Quizzes!

What does the common Italian gesture shown in the picture mean?

- Shall we go!
- Shut up!
- What are you saying??

Answer: What are you saying???

Are you *superstitious?*

Do you have a good luck charm?

Italians tend to be very superstitious … They believe that some things can bring good luck — and that other things cause bad luck! What do Italians say you must always carry with you for good luck?
A clue … It has the shape of a chili pepper!

- One tail
- One red glass
- One red *corno* ("horn")

Answer: One red corno. The corno originally represented a twisted animal horn.

And don't forget that in Italy, walking under a ladder is thought to bring bad luck … It's better to go around!

Palio di Siena

Italians are very proud of their traditions, and they hold huge events to remember and honor special dates in Italy's history.

One of the most important celebrations is the Palio di Siena. This was an ancient horse race that is still run today. It follows the same rules as it did eight centuries ago.

Palio di Siena takes place two times during the summer (on July 2 and August 16). The race and four-day celebration are held in the city of Siena, which is in Tuscany in central Italy. The people of Siena take the event very seriously. The rivalry is fierce because every horse in the race belongs to one of the city's districts (or *contrade* in Italian).

Did you know?
Sometimes the jockeys are thrown off of the horses, but even a horse without a jockey (called *cavallo scosso* in Italian) can win the race for its district!

The people of Siena say: *"Il palio dura tutto l'anno."* ("Palio lasts all year.") That's because they think about it and prepare for it all year long.

If a district doesn't win the race for many years, the Italians nickname it *Nonna.* (That means "Grandma" in Italian.)

One of the most talented people of all time: Leonardo da Vinci

Leonardo is very proud to introduce you to Leonardo da Vinci. He is known to be one of the most talented and intelligent people of all time. Leonardo da Vinci was an excellent artist, a great scientist, and a creative inventor!

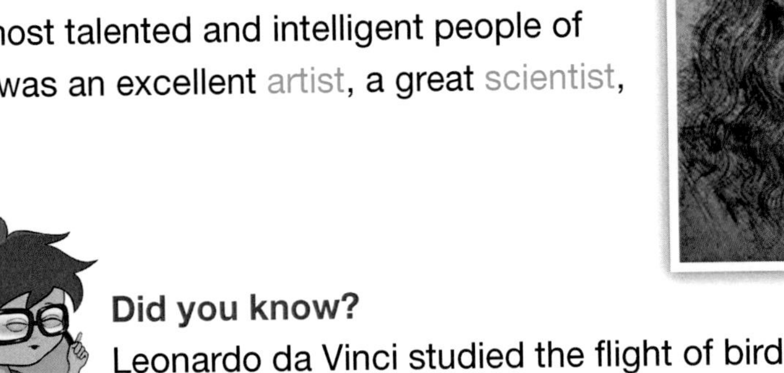

Did you know?
Leonardo da Vinci studied the flight of birds to draw plans for flying machines that resembled today's helicopters. But he couldn't build them because the technology needed didn't exist at that time.

Mirror writing

Leonardo da Vinci often wrote in the opposite direction to what is normal. This is called "mirror writing," because you need a mirror to read it! He may have written that way because he was left-handed — or because he wanted to hide his ideas from others.

Can you read this mirror writing?

Answer:
Leonardo is very smart!

Fun activity! Write a secret message in mirror writing and send it to your friends!

Did you know?
Leonardo da Vinci invented the first bicycle!

Leonardo da Vinci was a kind person! He liked to buy caged birds so he could set them free.

OUR Leonardo is also curious, smart, and an animal lover. He has made many new discoveries around the world that he likes to share with you. That's why our flying friend is named Leonardo too!

Other famous Italians you may know ...

Besides Leonardo da Vinci, many other Italians are world-famous for their accomplishments, including the artists **Michelangelo** and **Giotto**.

A famous leader ... meet Giuseppe Garibaldi

Many people tried to unite Italy into one kingdom. **Giuseppe Garibaldi** was the most popular leader of the struggle to unite the country. He and his soldiers fought successfully to unite Italy under the rule of one royal family (called House of Savoy).

The volunteers that followed Giuseppe Garibaldi in his battle wore shirts that were which color? (Hint: See Garibaldi's picture at right.)

- Green
- Red
- Purple

Answer:
Red

Did you know?

What is the fairy tale most loved by Italians? It's one you probably know: the story of **Pinocchio**, the wooden puppet who wants to become a real boy.

Quizzes!

What happens when Pinocchio tells a lie?

- He becomes short.
- His nose quickly grows.
- He loses his hand.

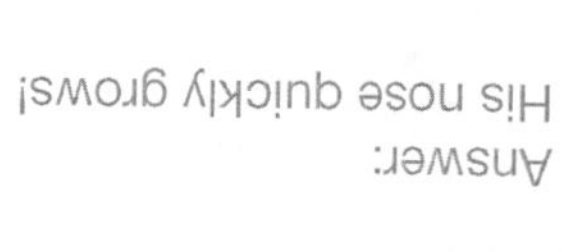

Answer:
His nose quickly grows!

Italian explorers and inventors ...

Italians are also famous for their inventions and discoveries.

Christopher Columbus was an Italian sailor who was born in the city of Genova. He wanted to find a better way to get to eastern Asia by sailing west around the world. He never knew that he had landed on a new continent instead: "The New World."

Quizzes!

What was the continent discovered by Columbus that was called "The New World"?

- Africa
- Asia
- America

Answer: America. This continent was named after the Italian explorer Amerigo Vespucci

Marco Polo was a merchant from Venice. He lived from 1254 to 1324. Marco Polo traveled a lot in order to trade goods. When he returned, he told the Italians about China and Indonesia — a part of the world that was unknown at that time.

Amerigo Vespucci was born in Florence in 1454. He sailed the same route as Columbus. But Amerigo Vespucci was the first explorer to realize that he hadn't landed in India, but in "The New World."

Did you know?

An Italian monk named Savino D'Armate invented eyeglasses in the 13th century. The eyeglasses sat on the nose, since frames weren't added until much later.

Italy is famous for ...

A leaning tower. It's not the Leaning Tower of Pizza — it's the Leaning Tower of Pisa (peeza). This marble tower was started in the year 1173, and took over 300 years to finish! But there was a problem ... The ground underneath the tower was too soft to support its weight. Shortly after it was built, the tower began to tilt. It now leans by almost 5 meters (more than 16 feet)!

Did you know?
There is a bell chamber at the top of the tower. Each bell is tuned to a note of the musical scale:
C, D, E, F, G, A, B
How many bells are there?

Answer: Seven

The most popular sport in Italy is football (soccer). Italy has won four World Cups — the last one was in 2006. What is the color of the national team and of the uniforms of the Italian athletes?

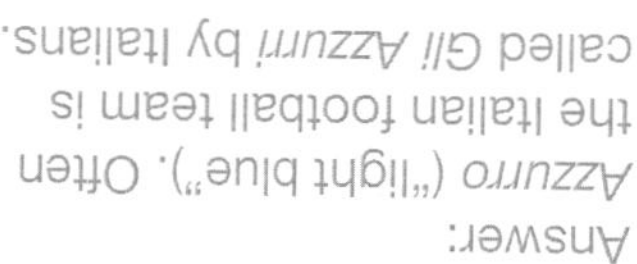

Answer:
Azzurro ("light blue"). Often the Italian football team is called *Gli Azzurri* by Italians.

Can you recognize this car? Hint: It's one of the famous sports cars produced in Italy.

Ferrari, along with Lamborghini, Alfa Romeo, and Maserati, are Italian luxury sports cars. They are used in car racing, where they can go over 200 mph! Ferrari is the most well-known Italian car manufacturer in the world.

More FUN FACTS about Italy!

Italy has the most hotel rooms of any European nation .

Sixty percent of all the world's art treasures are in Italy.

Italians eat 25 kg (55 lbs) of pasta per person every year. That's a lot of pasta!

Up and down ... Italy holds the Guinness record for having the most elevators.

The highest point in Italy is Mont Blanc, in the Alps. It's 4,807 meters (or almost 3 miles) high!

The longest river in Italy is the Po.

Over 75 percent of Italy is covered with mountains or hills.

The oldest olive tree in Italy grows in the Umbria region. It is said to be over 1,700 years old!

No other country in Europe has as many active volcanoes as Italy. The reason is that the Italian peninsula stands on a fault line. Three major volcanoes (Etna, Stromboli, and Vesuvius) have erupted in the last 100 years.

How do you say it in Italian ...?

A handy dictionary especially for you!

It's not hard to recognize the Italian language.

The pronunciation is soft and musical. That's why Italian is used for opera (a type of play where the words are sung instead of spoken).

Do you want to feel a little independent and speak some Italian yourself?

Here are a few common Italian words and how to pronounce them!

Did you know?
There are many local dialects (or differences in how things are said), depending on the region of the country.

Italian word	How does it sound?	What it means in English
Ciao	chow	Hello
Buon giorno	bwon zhor-no	Good morning
Buona sera	bwoh-nah say-rah	Good evening
Arrivederci	ah-ree-vuh-dehr-chee	Bye-bye/see you
Si	see	Yes
No	no	No
Prego	preh-goh	Please
Grazie	graht-zee-ay	Thank you
Grazie mille	graht-zee mee-lay	Thank you very much
Di niente	dee nee-ehn-teh	You're welcome
Scusa	skoo-zah	Excuse me
Mi dispiace	mee dee-spyah-cheh	Sorry
Non parlo Italiano	nohn par-lo ee-tahl-ee-ah-no	I do not speak Italian
Parli Inglese?	par-lee een-gleh-zay	Do you speak English?
Mi chiamo ___________.	mee kee-ah-mo	My name is ________.
Come ti chiami?	KOH-meh tee kee-AH-mee	What's your name?

Words to use at the restaurant ...

Family competition!
Who remembers more Italian words? Test each other ... The winner is the person who remembers at least five words with no mistakes!

Restaurant	Ristorante	ri-sto-ràn-te
Breakfast	Colazione	koh-lah-tsee-oh-nay
Lunch	Pranzo	prawn-tsoh
Dinner	Cena	che-nah
Milk	Latte	lah-tay
Bread	Pane	pah-nay
Cup	Tazza	tatz-zah
Glass	bicchiere	bik-kier-ay
Fork	Forchetta	for-ket-tah
Knife	Coltello	kol-tell-oh
Spoon	Cucchiaio	koo-chee-ya-choh
Sugar	Zucchero	sukh-keh-roh
Wine	Vino	vee-noh
Salt	Sale	saa-lay
Pepper	Pepe	pay-pay
Cake	Dolce	dole-chay
Honey	Miele	myeh-lay
Eggs	Uova	u-o-vah
Salad	Insalata	een-sah-lah-tah, een-sah-lah-teh
Beef	Vitello	vee-tehl-loh
Lamb	Agnello	ahn-nyel-loh
Pork	Maiale	mah-yah-lay
Steak	Bistecca	bee-steh-kah
Chicken	Pollo	pohl-loh
Noodles	Spaghetti	spah-geht-tee
Pasta	Pasta	pah-stah
Cheese	Formaggio	for-mah-joh
The bill	Il conto	ill kon-to
piece/slice	Pezzo/fetta	pett-so/feht-tah

Need to BUY something?

Learn Italian numbers!

One	Uno	Oo-noh
Two	Due	Doo-ay
Three	Tre	Tray
Four	Quattro	Kwaht-troh
Five	Cinque	Cheen-kway
Six	Sei	Say-ee
Seven	Sette	Set-tay
Eight	Otto	Oht-toh
Nine	Nove	Noh-vay
Ten	Dieci	Dee-ay-chee
One hundred	Cento	Chen-toh
One thousand	Mille	Meel-lay

Try to complete the sentences with the correct words in Italian:

There is ______________ (*one fork*) on the table, and I want to use it to eat __________________________ (*three pieces of cake, please*).

Answer: Una forchetta; tre pezzi di dolce, prego.

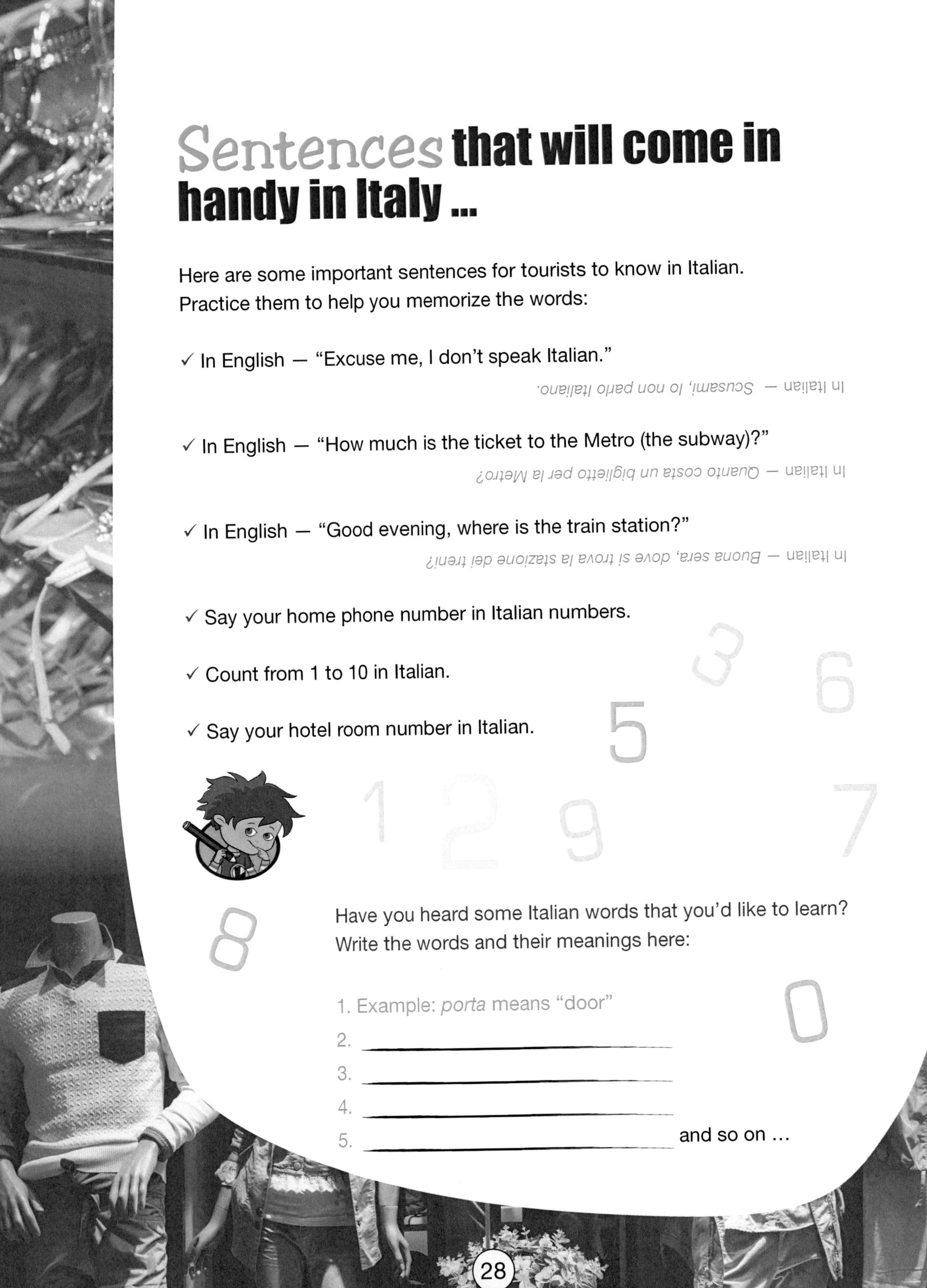

Sentences that will come in handy in Italy ...

Here are some important sentences for tourists to know in Italian. Practice them to help you memorize the words:

✓ In English — "Excuse me, I don't speak Italian."

In Italian — *Scusami, Io non parlo Italiano.*

✓ In English — "How much is the ticket to the Metro (the subway)?"

In Italian — *Quanto costa un biglietto per la Metro?*

✓ In English — "Good evening, where is the train station?"

In Italian — *Buona sera, dove si trova la stazione dei treni?*

✓ Say your home phone number in Italian numbers.

✓ Count from 1 to 10 in Italian.

✓ Say your hotel room number in Italian.

Have you heard some Italian words that you'd like to learn? Write the words and their meanings here:

1. Example: *porta* means "door"
2. ______________________________
3. ______________________________
4. ______________________________
5. ______________________________ and so on ...

What do you know about Italy?

1. On what continent is Italy located? ____________

2. Italy is shaped like what object? ____________

3. What natural border separates Italy from other countries in the north?
____

4. True or false? Po is the name of a river. ____________

5. What independent countries are located inside the boundaries of Italy? ____________

6. Where is the Vatican City? ____________

7. What is the Italian flag called? ____________

8. What colors appear on the Italian flag? What do the colors mean?
____

9. What type of money does Italy use? ____________

Answers:
1. Europe
2. Boot
3. Italian Alps
4. True
5. The Republic of San Marino and the Vatican City
6. In Rome
7. Tricolore
8. White, Red, and Green. White stands for Faith and the snow-capped Alps; Green for Hope and the plains; and Red for Charity and the blood shed to win Italy's independence.
9. Euro coins

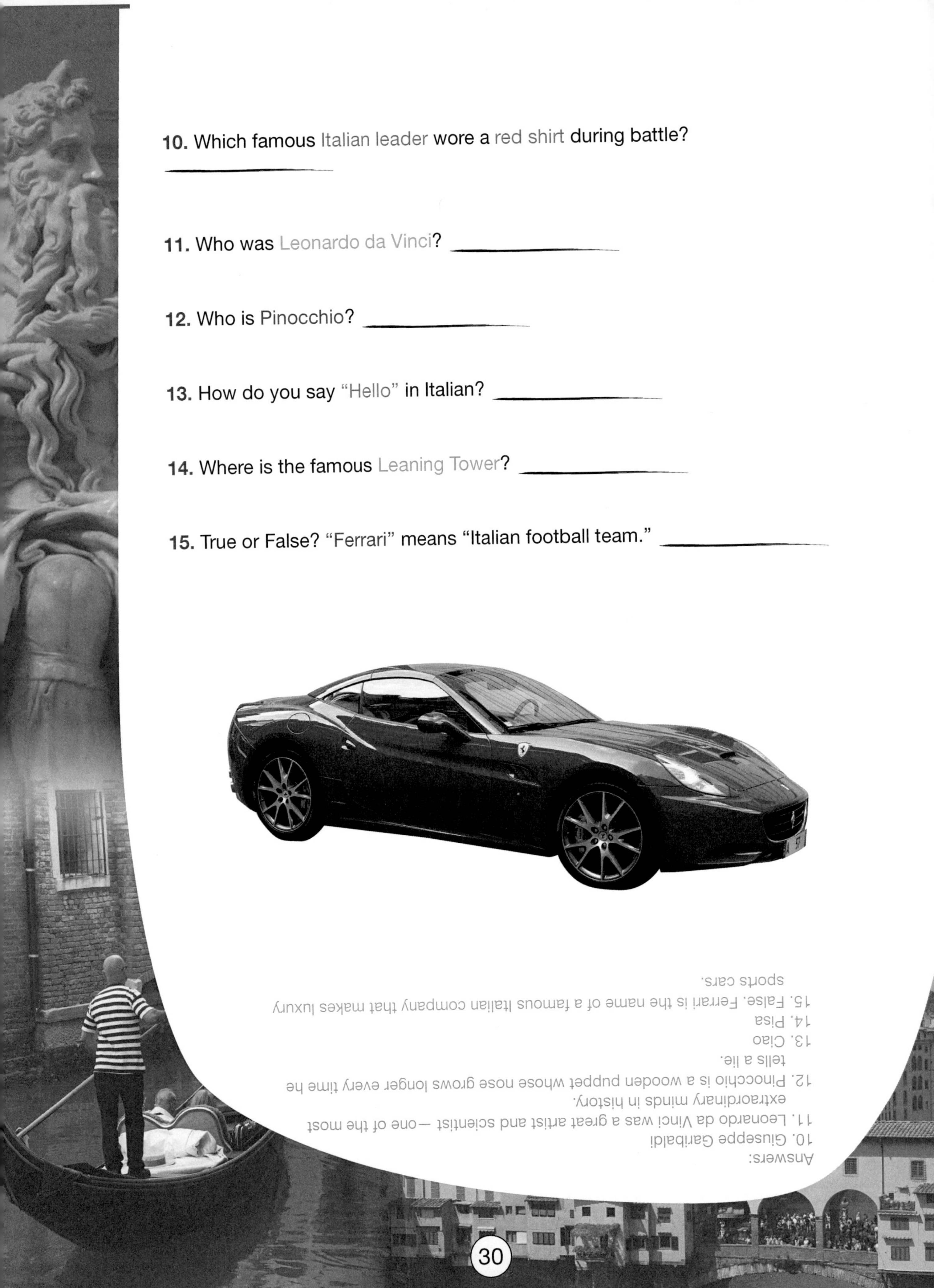

10. Which famous Italian leader wore a red shirt during battle? ____________

11. Who was Leonardo da Vinci? ____________

12. Who is Pinocchio? ____________

13. How do you say "Hello" in Italian? ____________

14. Where is the famous Leaning Tower? ____________

15. True or False? "Ferrari" means "Italian football team." ____________

Answers:
10. Giuseppe Garibaldi
11. Leonardo da Vinci was a great artist and scientist — one of the most extraordinary minds in history.
12. Pinocchio is a wooden puppet whose nose grows longer every time he tells a lie.
13. Ciao
14. Pisa
15. False. Ferrari is the name of a famous Italian company that makes luxury sports cars.

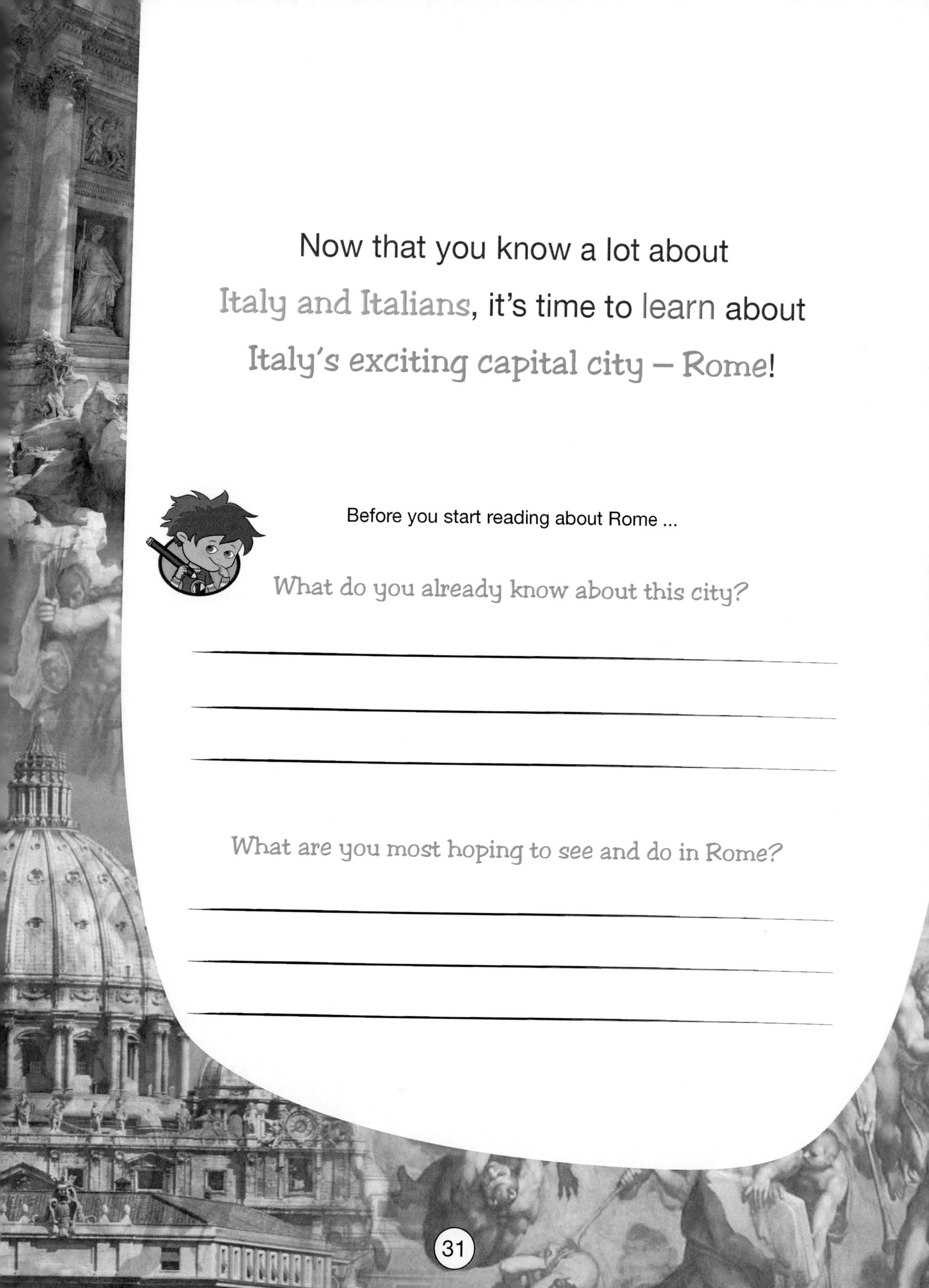

Now that you know a lot about Italy and Italians, it's time to learn about Italy's exciting capital city – Rome!

Before you start reading about Rome ...

What do you already know about this city?

___

___

___

What are you most hoping to see and do in Rome?

___

___

___

Welcome to Rome,
the Eternal City

Welcome to Rome, one of the world's most beautiful and fascinating cities! Rome is the capital of Italy. It's called the "Eternal City" because of its long life … over 2,500 years!

There is a lot to see … ready? You'll come across majestic ruins, awe-inspiring monuments, and amazing art! And it will be a thrill to discover the power of the ancient Roman Empire, because it had such a big influence on the world you live in today.

Why is Rome called Rome?

Romulus and his twin brother, Remus, were the children of a princess named Rhea Silvia and Mars, the god of war. Their greedy great-uncle abandoned them by the River Tiber, but a female wolf rescued them and fed them with her milk. When they grew up, they decided to build a city on the spot where the she-wolf had found them. But they had a fight about where it should be. Romulus killed Remus and then built the city, naming it after himself.

When you visit Rome, you will find the letters **'AD and BC'** after the dates on monuments. Do you remember what they mean?

AD is AFTER Jesus was born; BC is BEFORE Jesus was born.

Leonardo knows that the birth of Rome happened in 753 BC. How old was Rome in 2015?

- **753 years**
- **1,753 years**
- **2,768 years**

Answer: 2,768

Write your date of birth:

I was born ___________ AD/BC!

Did you know?

This statue is the symbol of Rome. It shows a wolf feeding the twins Romulus and Remus. It's called the **"Capitoline Wolf"** because it's located in the Capitoline Museum on the ancient Capitoline Hill.

More about Rome

Rome is also called **the Eternal City,** because of its long history. It was the home of the ancient Roman Empire. This huge empire ruled for more than 1,000 years. During that time, the empire spread its beliefs and practices throughout the known world.

In Rome, there are many monuments — like the Colosseum, the ancient Forum, and the temples. They recall Rome's glorious past. That's why Rome is also called … (Choose the right answer below):

- The open-air museum
- The virtual museum
- School every day

Answer:
Open-air museum

Quizzes!

Do you know which Italian city has the most people? A clue … It's also the capital!

- Milan
- Florence
- Rome

Answer: Rome, with a population of nearly three million.

Find the city of Rome on the map. Which sea is closest to Rome?

Answer: Tyrrhenian Sea

What does Rome look like?

Rome was built on seven hills. These hills are the oldest part of the city, and the most visited. You'll find a lot of the monuments there.

A long river crosses the city and then divides into two parts. It flows under many beautiful bridges, and it even has a little island. Do you know the name of this river? You can take a look at the map for a clue ...

Answer: Tiber

Quizzes! **What is the name of the island that sits in the river?**

Answer: Tiber Island

Did you know?
The Vatican City, inside the city of Rome, has the smallest population of any country in the world. Only 800 people live there!

Can you help Leonardo find all seven hills in Rome?

- Aventine Hill
- Caelian Hill
- Capitoline Hill
- Esquiline Hill
- Palatine Hill
- Quirinal Hill
- Viminal Hill

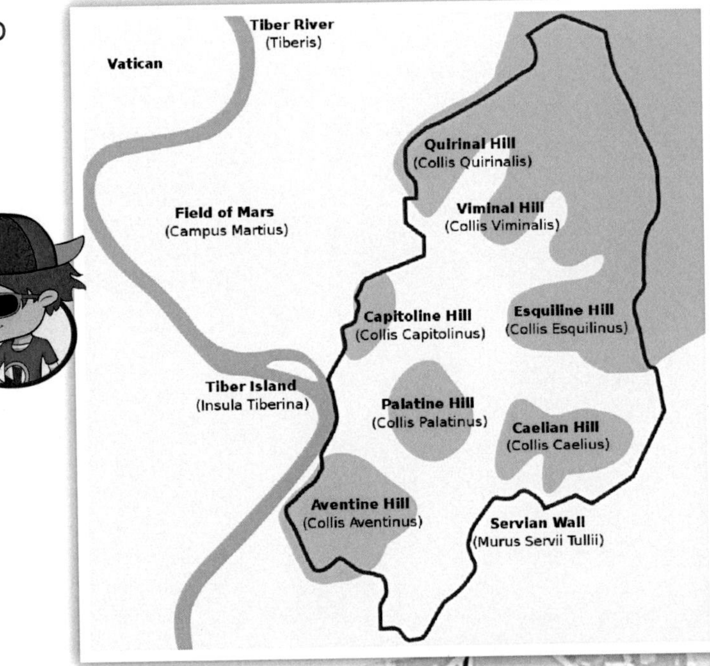

Things to see only in Rome!

Rome is the ideal place to wander around. It's an amazing space where you can touch really ancient times — and feel like an ancient gladiator! So let's go ... There is so much to see in Rome! But don't worry — Leonardo will tell you about all the things you don't want to miss!

Here are a few fun things to do in Rome:

- **Throw a coin into the Trevi Fountain: Make a wish, and then use your right hand to toss the coin over your left shoulder. Remember — your back has to be to the fountain if you want your wish to come true!**
- **Visit the Colosseum, one of the Seven Wonders of the World! You'll be impressed by the greatness of the place where ancient gladiators fought.**
- **Enjoy fantastic views of ancient monuments, and imagine yourself as a powerful and triumphant emperor.**
- **Taste Italian ice cream (called "gelato") or a slice of pizza during your walks ... There are so many different kinds of food in Italy that Leonardo hasn't finished discovering them all yet!**
- **Try to speak in Italian, using the Italian words you learned on pages 25–28.**

Ciao! Mi chiamo Leonardo.

Help Leonardo remember how to pronounce these Italian phrases:

- *Buon giorno* → *(Good morning)*
- *Buona sera* → *(Good evening)*
- *Grazie* → *(Thank you)*

And here's a new one:

- *Per favore* → *sounds like:* **pear fa-vor-reh** *(Can I have...)*

Rome's special language — symbols and signs ...

There are a lot of symbols (lions, dragons, stars, trees, and many others) carved into all the monuments in Rome.
Every symbol has its special meaning! But they were all created to show the power of the Roman Empire and its victories and superiority.

The most famous slogan in Rome!

You'll find this slogan all over the city.
The letters *SPQR* mean *Senatus Populusque Romanus* in Latin, or "the Senate and the people of Rome."

Quizzes!

What was the animal symbol for military power in Rome?

Panther
Eagle
Lion
Wolf
Boar

Answer: Eagle

Did you know?

What kind of crown did the **emperor wear**?
Not a crown made of gold or silver or precious gems! The emperor wore a crown of laurel leaves, a symbol of the highest honor!

Find a laurel plant and build your own **crown**!
Now people will think that You are a very important person!

VIA DEL CORSO

PIGNA

We can't really meet Rome without knowing a little bit about its history ...

The ROMAN EMPIRE — a great history!

Have you heard the saying *"Rome wasn't built in a day"*? ... Well, its long life is an amazing story!

In 753 BC, Rome was a little village on the River Tiber that was ruled by the Etruscans (people from the center of Italy). But Rome became a republic when a revolt against King Tarquin the Proud ended the Etruscans' power.

The Roman Republic was the most powerful city in the Mediterranean area. It spread its practices and its example of democracy to others.
Julius Caesar was the last leader of the republic. He was definitely the most famous leader in the history of ancient Rome!

Julius Caesar was a powerful general who greatly helped to expand the boundaries of Rome.

He was born in 100 BC, and he began his career when he was still a teenager. He conquered all of the land that is now France and Belgium, and he invaded Britain twice.

At that time, the Roman Empire was a democratic republic. But Julius Caesar became so powerful that he made himself the master of Rome. In 44 BC, he was killed by people who wanted to free Rome from his control.

From *Caesar* to the emperors ...

Did you know?
The month of July was named to honor Julius Caesar. While Caesar was the master of Rome, he created the calendar we use today! He made the year 365 days long, with 366 days in leap years. He decided to start the year with the month of January.

Veni, vidi, vici: These are the famous Latin* words that Julius Caesar used to describe one of his fastest victories.
What do they mean?

- I came, I saw, I conquered.
- I played, I ate, I slept.
- I dreamt, I woke up, I sneezed.

Answer: I came, I saw, I conquered.

Did you know?
Julius Caesar was the first person to have his head put on a Roman coin.

After Caesar's death, the new leader, **Octavian Augustus**, was called the emperor, and the Roman Empire began. It was the biggest empire in the world for over four centuries. Its power extended everywhere.

This is a statue of the first emperor of Rome, **Augustus**.
Pay attention to the pose of the emperor:
You'll see many Roman statues in this position.
The right arm is raised to show the authority and power of the person.

Try to find at least one statue with this pose in Rome ...
Where did you find it?

____

____

If you save pictures of all the statues you see in this pose, you'll create a collection of Roman emperors!

*Latin was the language spoken during the time of the Roman Empire.

The fall of Rome and the power of the POPES

The Roman Empire began to get weaker when the Barbarians attacked.

Have you ever heard of the Barbarians?

They were tribes of people living outside the Roman Empire. They didn't speak Latin, and the Romans thought their language sounded like "bar-bar-bar." That's why the Romans called them "barbarians."

In the medieval period,* Rome lost its power. But during the Renaissance, the Catholic Popes wanted to make Rome important again. So they decided to fill the city with magnificent new monuments. These monuments were built to show the Pope's power and the superiority of the Catholic Church.

Did you know?

***The medieval** period, or Middle Ages, started with the fall of the Roman Empire around 400 AD. It ended with the **Renaissance**. Do you remember what Renaissance means? **Rebirth.**

The city of Rome was part of the Catholic Church until 1870. That's when **Rome became the capital of Italy, which it still is today!**

Quizzes!

Do you know the name of the current Pope?

____

Where does he live? ________________

Answers:
Pope Francis
He lives in Vatican City.

Let's go! How to get around in Rome

Use your feet ... Walking in Rome is a wonderful experience, since amazing monuments and beautiful buildings are all around ...

No matter what kind of transportation you and your family choose, Leonardo wants to remind you that **Rome is built on seven hills**. So make sure you have comfortable shoes to wear!

Option #1

The easiest and fastest way to get around in Rome is the subway. It gets you to all the major attractions easily. There are two lines: Line **A**, the red line, and Line B, the blue line. Their entrances are shown by a large red sign marked with an **M**.

You can tell your parents that if you are under age 10, you don't need to pay a fare — you can travel free with an adult!

Use this map to help your family organize your route!
The subway lines make a rough X.

Leonardo visited the Colosseum, and now he wants to go to the Spanish Steps (Spagna). **Can you** help him plan his route using the subway? What is the color of the line he's on now? How many stations is it to the Spanish Steps?

Answer: To reach the Spanish Steps — Spagna — Leonardo has to take the blue line to Termini (central station), and then the red line for three stops.

Option #2

The other way to travel around Rome is by **bus**. There are many routes available, but buses are often very crowded.

The most popular bus line is 40 Express. It connects the center of Rome to the Vatican and St. Peter's Square. **Don't expect an orderly line!**

Option #3

You can also get on a **tourist bus.** The **110 OPEN is a special double-decker red bus** that goes to some of the most famous sights — like the Colosseum, Piazza Navona, and St. Peter's Square.

This bus lets you **hop on and hop off** at any of the stops for the whole day.

You'll get wonderful photos and video from the OPEN Bus!

There is another way to travel in Rome — by horse-drawn carriage! Have you ever taken a carriage ride?

How would you most like to get around in Rome? ______________________

Which kind of transportation is your family going to use in Rome?

____

It's time to eat in Rome!

Have you heard about Italian food? Well ... Leonardo has a lot of fantastic foods to tell you about!

Italy probably has more different dishes than any place in the world. You'll surely want to taste the pasta, pizza, and gelato ... But you'll find that it's difficult to choose with so many types of food!

Did you know?
There are more than 1,000 kinds of pizza in Italy? Let's go discover some of them!

Pizza was invented in the city of Naples around 1860. A baker named Raffaele Esposito prepared the first type of pizza to honor the Queen of Italy at that time — Margherita di Savoia. He made the pizza with ingredients that were the same colors as the Italian flag. He named his pizza Margherita, after the Queen. Help Leonardo find which ingredients match the colors of the Italian flag.

White is ____________________

Red is ____________________

Green is ____________________

Answers:
Mozzarella is white.
Tomatoes are red.
Basil is green.

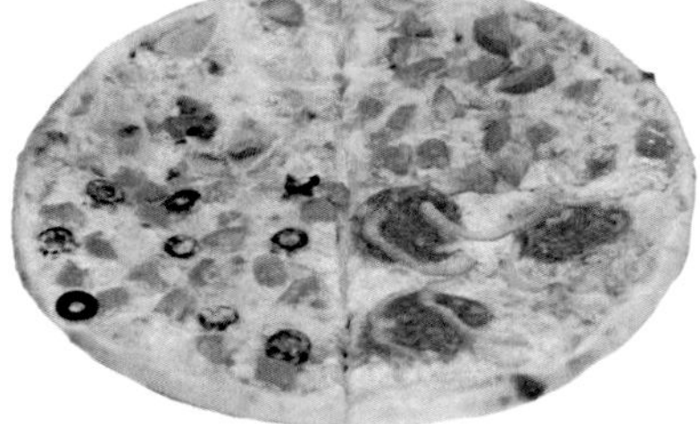

The base for Italian pizza is a **very thin** flat bread. It is loaded with fresh vegetables or thinly sliced ham or salami. Other popular toppings are artichokes, garlic, tomatoes, or olives. There are even pizzas topped with eggs! The pizzas are **baked in a wood-fired oven.**

What is a shop where you can buy pizza called?
A *pizzeria*! Here you can sit and eat a circle pizza. If you want to eat some pizza while you are walking, you have to ask for a slice of pizza at a *pizzerie al taglio*. That's a shop that sells pizza in slices.

Ready to learn about different kinds of pizza? Mmm ...

Leonardo's mouth is watering!

Here are some famous kinds of pizza with their ingredients. Can you match each type of pizza with the right picture? Look at the ingredients shown in the photos!

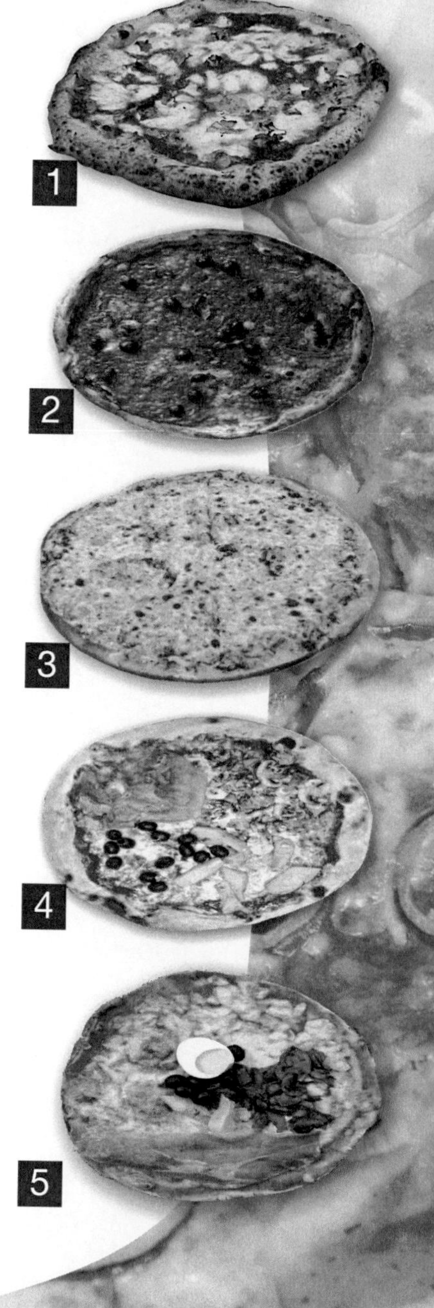

A. Pizza Marinara
Ingredients: Oil, tomato, garlic, and oregano. It is named "marinara" because it was originally taken along on voyages so that sailors (or *marinai*) could eat pizza during the journey.

B. Pizza Napoletana (Naples)
Ingredients: Tomatoes, mozzarella, anchovies, and capers.

C. Pizza Capricciosa
Ingredients: Mushrooms, ham, artichoke hearts, olives, and half of a hard-boiled egg.

D. Pizza Quattro Stagioni (Pizza Four Seasons)
The ingredients are divided into four sections, one for each season: Spring (olives and artichokes); summer (peppers); autumn (tomato and mozzarella); winter (mushrooms and hard-boiled eggs).

E. Pizza Ai Quattro Formaggi (Pizza with Four Cheeses)
Ingredients: Mozzarella and three local cheeses, such as Gorgonzola, ricotta, and parmigiano-reggiano.

Answers: A-2; B-1; C-5; D-4; E-3

Don't forget to try Italian spaghetti!

Look at this picture ... Yes, it's a fabulous dish of spaghetti — the most well-known type of pasta in Italy.

Pasta is an ancient food, made with four simple ingredients: water, flour, semolina (hard grains left after flour is milled), and salt.

Sometimes eggs are added to create *pasta all'uovo* ("pasta with eggs"). This is common in the northern part of Italy.

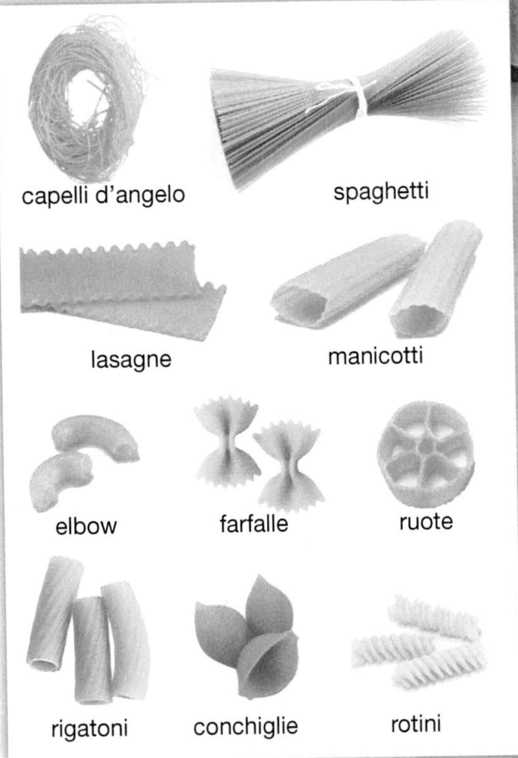

What is the right way to eat spaghetti?

It's not easy to eat spaghetti using only a fork, but that's the Italian way — and you can learn it! Simply pick up the right amount of spaghetti, roll it around on your fork, and reach your mouth as soon as possible 😉 !

Help Leonardo connect the pictures to the right type of Italian pasta shown above!

Tip! You can use pasta to create dazzling jewelry. Put the pasta (for example, rigatoni) into a ziplock bag with food coloring. Close the bag and shake it until the pasta is colored. Take the pasta out of the bag and let it dry on a paper towel. After that, you can use the pasta for your creations! Put it on a string to make a colorful necklace or bracelet!

Will you be able to eat it BEFORE IT MELTS?

What is another tasty Italian delight that you can't miss? Some hints:

- It's not hot.
- It is made of milk.
- It's frozen.

Quizzes!

Answer: It's gelato!

There are several types of gelato, with many different flavors to choose from, such as fresh fruit, chocolate, and hazlenut!

Gelato is served in a cone or in a cup. You can get up to FOUR flavors in one cone! But be careful not to stain your clothes — G ____________ O melts very fast!

Do you prefer a cone or a cup? Why?

____

You can ask for a gelato in special shops called *gelateria* in Italian. You'll see all the flavors of gelato you can choose right in the shop window.

There is another frozen dessert Italians love: *granita*! It's made of coarse ice, sugar, and flavorings. And you don't need to worry about stains: you drink it with a straw …

The foods I ate in Italy ...

What is your favorite Italian food?

____

Have you ever tasted it before?

____

Paste a picture of your favorite Italian food here as a souvenir!

Quizzes!

If you went with Leonardo to an Italian restaurant, which of these foods would you be most likely to find on the menu?

- ✓ Cheeseburgers
- ✓ Spaghetti
- ✓ Fish and Chips

Answer: Spaghetti

Pizza is made with this basic ingredient:

- ✓ Rice
- ✓ Flat bread
- ✓ Meat

Answer: Flat bread

What is the food you can eat in a cone or in a cup?

- ✓ Gelato
- ✓ Rigatoni
- ✓ Pizza

Answer: Gelato

Leonardo has just landed in Italy, and he wants to taste some new foods.
Can you help him?

1. Where can he find a slice of pizza?
2. Where can he eat a dish of spaghetti?
3. Where can he taste a gelato?

Answers:
1. Pizzeria
2. Ristorante, or osteria or trattoria
3. Gelateria

The whole city in your hands!

Would you like to see the whole city from one spot?
Well ... it's possible! Rome has lots of places to visit, but if you want to see it all at once, ask your family to go to one of these high places where you can view the entire city!

Janiculum Hill — hear the cannon go off at noon!

On this green hill high above the Vatican, you can admire a beautiful view of Rome. Every day at noon, a soldier fires a cannon to announce that it's midday.

Vittoriano Monument

Go to the terrace on the roof of the huge Vittoriano Complex. You'll be able to see the whole spectacular landscape of Rome! (Vittoriano Complex is near the ancient Forum in Venezia Square.)

Did you know?

Vittoriano Monument was built to honor Victor Emanuel, the first King of Italy. Find the statue of him on his horse!

Dome of St. Peter

From the beautiful dome of St. Peter's Basilica you can enjoy a 360° view of Rome. Try to find the River Tiber crossing Rome!

See whether you can recognize the Colosseum and other sights from the viewpoints you visit!

In Rome, there are many churches with domes ... How many domes can you count from every viewpoint?

- Two
- More than four
- Less than ten
- More than ten
- Between three and twelve

The ROMAN FORUM: imagine you were ...

The Roman Forum was the heart and soul of ancient Rome. It was the public square where Romans did their banking, trading, shopping, chatting, and praying ... Today, it is a huge archeological* site. The remains are called "ruins." Here you can see what's left of Rome's great past! Let's go discover it!

*Archeologists study the remains of ancient buildings and objects.

Did you know?
Forum is a Latin word meaning "open space" or "marketplace."

Let's start with the main road! Can you recognize it?
A clue ... it begins at an arch ...

The main road of the Forum is called **the Sacred Way** (or *Via Sacra*). It begins at the **Arch of Titus.** This arch was built in 80 AD to celebrate the victories of Emperor Titus against the Jews in Israel.

Did you know?
Arches were built to remember the most important victories and to honor the emperors ... The big battles were fought far away from Rome. When the victorious emperor returned, huge celebrations were held in the Forum!

On the Via Sacra, you'll find another large arch built for an emperor ...
The Arch of Septimius Severus!

Notice the differences between these arches!

Which arch is bigger? ____________________

What can you read above both arches? ____________________

Which one is the most ancient? ____________________

Exploring **the Forum ...**

Stand with your back to the Septimius Severus Arch and your face toward the main road. What do you see on the left? Do you see the big building with three windows above the door?

This brick building is the **Curia** or **Senate House**. The leaders of ancient Rome met here to make decisions about governing the city. The Curia was built by Julius Caesar. In the seventh century AD, the Curia was turned into a church. Many other monuments in the Forum became churches too.

Find another monument in the Forum that was made into a church! Leonardo has a clue: you can count **10 columns** in front of the church!

____

Next to the Curia is **the Rostra.** On this half-circle platform, the great Roman orators (public speakers) gave their speeches. Crowds of people gathered to listen. Leonardo wants you to pretend you are Julius Caesar and make a speech from the Rostra!

You can announce to your family all your plans for tomorrow: you will wake up at ________ o'clock, and you'll eat a gelato with

____

Answer: The Temple of Antonio and Faustina, now the Chruch of San Lorenzo in Miranda, is located near the ruins of the Basilica Aemilia. See the map on page 22!

THE TEMPLES — places of power and gods

In ancient Rome, people believed in many gods. They built magnificent temples to thank the gods. The people hoped this would bring them protection and luck.

Near the Rostra, you'll see one of the oldest and most sacred places in Rome — the giant Temple of Saturn. The Roman State Treasury was inside. It stored bronze, silver, and gold. (Find the picture on the next page.)

Quizzes!

How many columns does the Temple of Saturn have?

10
5
8

Look at this picture: it's the **Temple of Vesta**. Here the Vestal Virgins (priestesses) tended a sacred fire so the flame would never go out. Each Vestal Virgin was picked when she was between 6 and 10 years old. They had to serve and remain virgins for 30 years. After that, they could get married. Vestal Virgins were very honored. They had rights that other women didn't.

Try to find the Temple of Vesta! Leonardo has a clue … It is semi-circular, and it's near the Temple of Castor and Pollux, which has only three pillars still remaining …

Who were Castor and Pollux?

They were mythological twin brothers. A legend says they helped Rome defeat the Etruscan King Tarquinius Superbus. Their temple was built at the spot in the Forum where the victory was announced.

Did you know?

In 20 BC, Emperor Augustus built a tall column — called the **Milliarium Aureum** — in front of the Temple of Saturn. The distance to every place in the Roman Empire was measured by starting at this column. Try to find its remains!

Do you know how far it is from your country or your city to Rome?

____

Who were the gods of ancient Rome?

Well, there were a lot of them! Do you know how many gods the ancient Romans worshipped?

- More than 20
- Less than 76
- More than 300

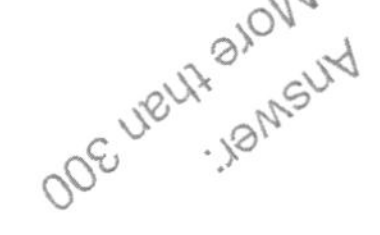

The Romans took many of their gods from the Greeks. They just changed their names. Roman gods were a lot like humans. But the gods had special powers, and they were immortal. They had families and special personalities. They could be moody or cruel or loving. People believed the gods took care of and protected those who honored them.

Who was the king of all the gods? A clue: it's also the biggest **planet** in our solar system!

- Jupiter
- Romulus
- The Pope

Did you know?
In ancient Rome, it was possible for a person to become a god. Many emperors and members of their families were turned into gods.

Juno was Jupiter's sister and also his wife!
She was the queen of the gods.
Juno protected Roman women.

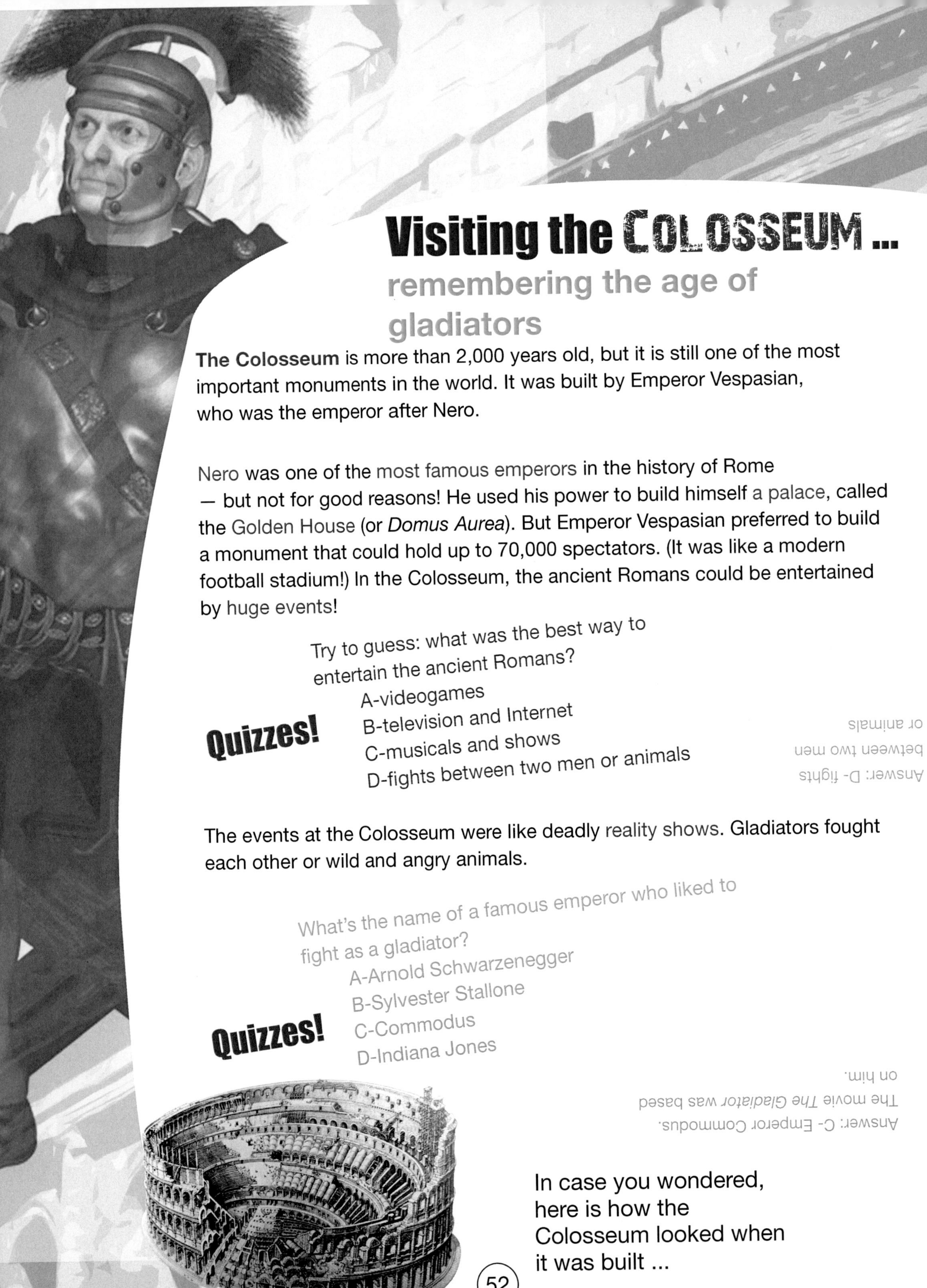

Visiting the COLOSSEUM ...

remembering the age of gladiators

The Colosseum is more than 2,000 years old, but it is still one of the most important monuments in the world. It was built by Emperor Vespasian, who was the emperor after Nero.

Nero was one of the most famous emperors in the history of Rome — but not for good reasons! He used his power to build himself a palace, called the Golden House (or *Domus Aurea*). But Emperor Vespasian preferred to build a monument that could hold up to 70,000 spectators. (It was like a modern football stadium!) In the Colosseum, the ancient Romans could be entertained by huge events!

Quizzes!

Try to guess: what was the best way to entertain the ancient Romans?

A-videogames
B-television and Internet
C-musicals and shows
D-fights between two men or animals

Answer: D- fights between two men or animals

The events at the Colosseum were like deadly reality shows. Gladiators fought each other or wild and angry animals.

Quizzes!

What's the name of a famous emperor who liked to fight as a gladiator?

A-Arnold Schwarzenegger
B-Sylvester Stallone
C-Commodus
D-Indiana Jones

Answer: C- Emperor Commodus. The movie *The Gladiator* was based on him.

In case you wondered, here is how the Colosseum looked when it was built ...

What was the *life* of a GLADIATOR like?

Who were the gladiators?

Gladiators were the professional fighters of ancient Rome. They were often criminals or slaves. Even though they weren't free, they could become famous — just like sports stars today. Gladiators were forced to fight. They lived in a special school close to the Colosseum, where they trained constantly. You have probably seen some movies about gladiators ...

Did you know?
"Gladiator" comes from the Latin word *gladius*, which means "sword."

And what happened when a gladiator wanted to stop fighting?
After losing a fight, the gladiator's life depended on a vote by the crowd — thumbs up or thumbs down.

Did you know?
Most gladiators were men, but there were some women fighters too.

Quizzes!

There were different types of Roman gladiators, and each group had different gear and weapons. Find your gladiator ... Circle the letter that describes the gladiator in the picture!

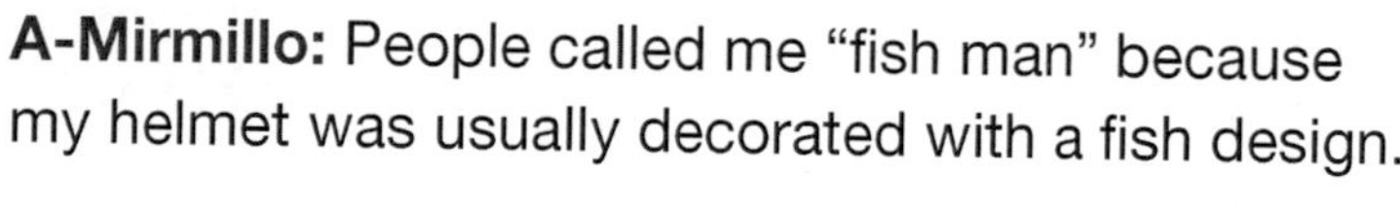

A-Mirmillo: People called me "fish man" because my helmet was usually decorated with a fish design.

B-Secutor: I wear a helmet with two small, round eye holes.

C-Thracian: I fought with a curved sword and strong body armor.

Answer:
A-Mirmillo

Discovering the secrets of the Colosseum!

The Colosseum is full of underground passages called **hypogeum**. Here, the animals and gladiators waited under the floor. They were brought up to the arena by special devices. These were designed so the gladiators could come charging out of trapdoors and surprise the people.

Where did the name Colosseum come from?
It's original name was *Amphitheatrum Flavium*. **But it probably became known as** the Colosseum because it was near a giant statue of Nero called *Colosso*.

People could go to the Colosseum for free. They were given cards with numbers that told them where to sit. If you look above the Colosseum's remaining arches, you can still see the numbers that matched the cards.

Did you know?
In ancient Rome, numbers were written as letters of the alphabet!

What numbers match the following Roman numerals?

XXII
XXXVI
XVII
VI

Answers:
22
36
17
6

ROMAN NUMERALS

1	I	20	XX
2	II	30	XXX
3	III	40	XL
4	IV	50	L
5	V	60	LX
6	VI	70	LXX
7	VII	80	LXXX
8	VIII	90	XC
9	IX	100	C
10	X	500	D
		1000	M

St. Peter's Basilica
and its treasure!

Saint Peter's Basilica is the world's largest church. It is famous for its magnificence! A legend says it was built where **St. Peter** was buried. He was the first disciple, or follower, of Jesus Christ.

The Basilica is in **Vatican City** — the miniature country inside Rome. It's the home of the **Pope,** who is the head of the Roman Catholic Church.

What is the first thing you need to do when you get to St. Peter's Basilica?
Well ... you need to pass through St. Peter's **Square.** This huge space was built by the famous architect Bernini. It is bordered by grand colonnades (rows of columns). They are meant to symbolize a big embrace for all the people of the world.

What is located in the center of the square?

- A lion
- An obelisk
- The seat of the Pope

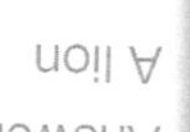

Answer: A lion

Can you guess how many statues of saints and martyrs stand on top of the colonnades?

Do you remember how big Vatican City is? Only 0.44 square km (0.17 square miles).

Answer: 140 statues

Help Leonardo find the Pope's window!

Every Sunday **from this window**, the Pope gives his welcome to the crowd that comes to St. Peter's Square. It is the second window from the right on the top floor ... Find it and take a picture!

St. Peter's Basilica — *let's go inside!*

And what's inside the Basilica?
The Basilica is decorated with beautiful monuments that show the power of the Catholic Church. The most famous one is the *Pietà*. It's a sculpture carved in marble by **Michelangelo.** It shows Mary's sorrow as she holds the dead body of Jesus.
This is the only statue by Michelangelo that has his signature.

Michelangelo is one of greatest artists of all times. He was born in Tuscany on March 6, 1475, but he spent most of his life in Rome. He worked as an architect, painter, and sculptor for Pope Julius II. Michelangelo showed great talent even when he was very young!

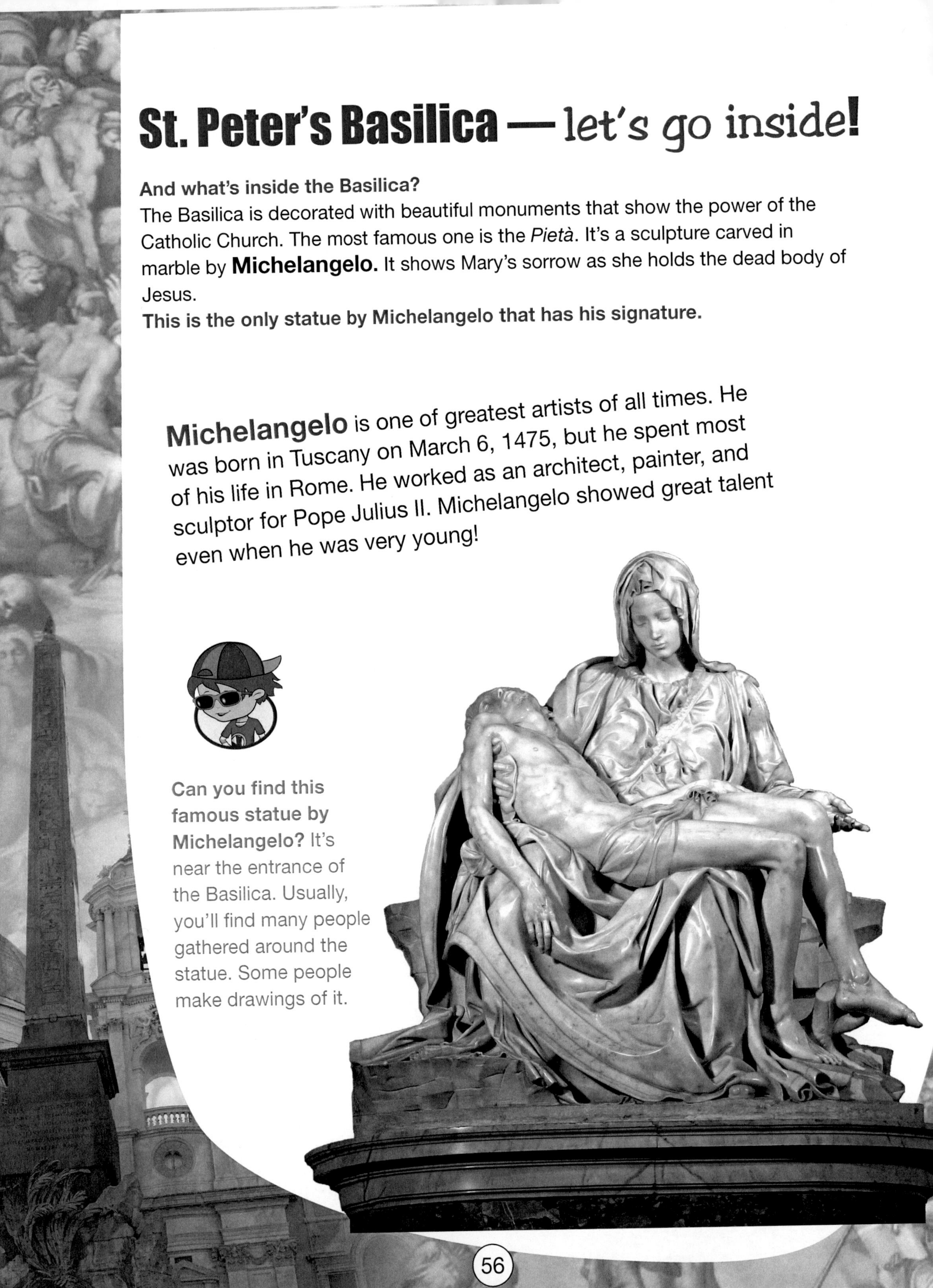

Can you find this famous statue by Michelangelo? It's near the entrance of the Basilica. Usually, you'll find many people gathered around the statue. Some people make drawings of it.

MICHELANGELO and the Sistine Chapel

Michelangelo is the creator of the majestic dome on **St. Peter's Basilica.**
It's huge — 42.34 meters (or almost 140 feet)!
Do you remember when Leonardo told you about great places to view the whole city? Well, this is one of the places!!!

The **Sistine Chapel** is the most famous sight in the Vatican Museum. You'll find it at the end of the Museum tour.

Did you know?

The chapel is named for Pope Sixtus IV. He had the chapel built in the 15th century AD.

Leonardo has discovered some big numbers for the Sistine Chapel:

- About 25,000 people a day, or 5 million people a year, visit the chapel.
- The chapel's paintings cover 1,110 square meters (12,000 square feet).
- Over 300 figures are painted on the chapel's ceiling.

What is the important event that still takes place in **the Sistine Chapel?**

When the **Pope** dies or retires, the Cardinals from all over the world come here to choose a new Pope. At a special meeting called a "conclave," every Cardinal casts his secret vote. They keep voting until someone gets enough votes to be the new Pope.
After every vote, either black or white smoke is sent up the chimney. The color lets people know whether a new Pope has been elected or not.
What color of smoke **announces the election of the new Pope**? Black or white?

Answer: White

Inside the Sistine Chapel

Look at the beautiful frescoes* painted on the walls and ceiling of the Sistine Chapel. Famous artists like Botticelli did the paintings on the walls. But the scenes on the ceiling are the most impressive and well-known. Michelangelo painted them in 1508.

***Fresco** means "fresh" in Italian. The artist paints directly on the fresh, wet plaster of a wall.

Painting a fresco is very difficult. Can you think why? The painter has to complete the work before the paint dries ... and no mistakes are allowed. Otherwise, the artist has to start over from the beginning!

Did you know?

Michelangelo liked sculpting more than anything. In the beginning, he didn't want to paint the Sistine Chapel. He only did it because Pope Julius II forced him to.

The Sistine Chapel's frescoes describe nine stories from the Christian Bible's book of Genesis.

Leonardo suggests that you use a mirror to see the ceiling better without hurting your neck!

Can you find the most famous painting in the center of the ceiling?

It shows the most important moment, **the creation of Adam,** the first man created by God!

Leonardo suggests you look at this painting carefully. Can you find a brain in *The Creation of Adam* scene? Where?

Trevi Fountain ...

see the King of the Sea

Trevi Fountain (*Fontana di Trevi*) is the largest and most famous **baroque** fountain in Italy.

What is "baroque"?

Baroque art is very fancy and elaborate, with lots of ornaments. It was very popular In Europe in the 17th century. In Rome, you'll find lots of statues and fountains in the baroque style. Do you want to impress your family? Leonardo will help you recognize this style so you can tell your family what they are viewing!

Trevi Fountain is located at the end of the ancient aqueduct, or channel, called Aqua Virgo. It provided water for the thermal (hot) baths. The baths were very popular in ancient Rome ... kind of like swimming pools are today!

Guess how big **Trevi Fountain is!**

A - 25.9 meters high and 19.8 meters wide (about 85 feet high and 65 feet wide)
B - 200 meters high and 1 meter wide (about 656 feet high and 3-1/4 feet wide)
C - 1 meter high and 300 meters wide (3-1/4 feet high and 984 feet wide)

Answer: A - 25.9 meters high and 19.8 meters wide (about 85 feet high and 65 feet wide)

So what do you see ...? Discover the fountain with Leonardo and choose the right answers!

In the center is a big statue representing the King of the Sea:

- Oceanus
- Spiderman
- Superman

He is riding a chariot in the shape of a shell. On either side of him there is a triton (a sea god or goddess) and a

- Turtle
- Butterfly
- Horse

Answers:
Horse
Oceanus

Trevi Fountain ...
make a wish!

Have you heard of Neptune? He came after Oceanus, and he was called the God of the Sea. Can you see an important difference between Oceanus and Neptune? Leonardo suggests you look carefully at the two of them below! What is the difference?

Answer: Neptune is holding a three-pronged spear called a "trident."

Leonardo wondered ... What do the Colosseum and Trevi Fountain have in common? Do you know the answer?

Answer: They were built with the same type of marble!

Find a nice place to sit with your family and color the picture of Neptune.

Did you know?

A legend says that if you throw a coin into Trevi Fountain, you are sure to come back to Rome. More than 3,000 euros (or over $4,000 US dollars) in coins are tossed into the fountain every day!

Piazza Navona ...

see Neptune's fountain and much more!

Welcome to **Piazza Navona!** Take a look around you.
What do you see in Piazza Navona?

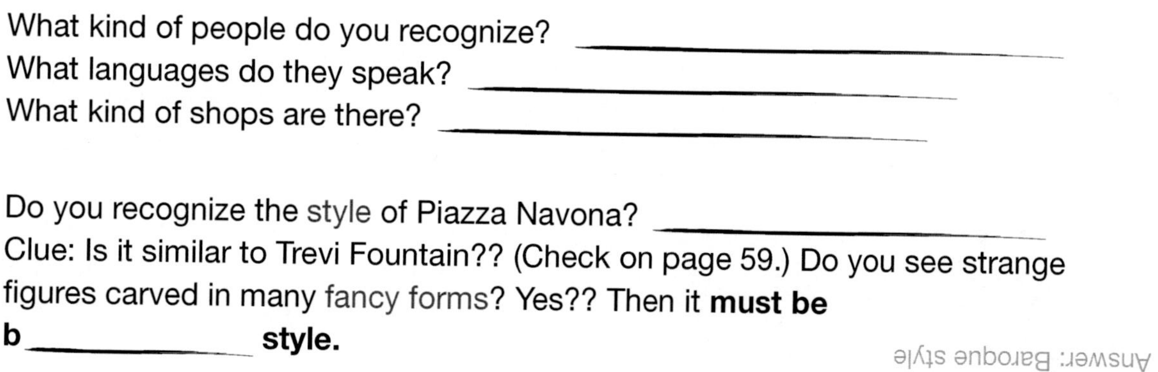

What kind of people do you recognize? ______________________
What languages do they speak? ______________________
What kind of shops are there? ______________________

Do you recognize the style of Piazza Navona? ______________________
Clue: Is it similar to Trevi Fountain?? (Check on page 59.) Do you see strange figures carved in many fancy forms? Yes?? Then it **must be b__________ style.**

Answer: Baroque style

Did you know?

Fights and chariot races were held in this square for many centuries.

In ancient Rome, going to chariot races was even more popular than watching gladiators! The chariots had two wheels and were pulled by horses. Some chariot drivers started training when they were just children. And many star drivers were teenagers.

You'll see Neptune with his trident in the fountain on the north side of the square. But you'll find the biggest fountain in the center of **Piazza Navona** – the Fountain of Four Rivers. Bernini built it. (He's the one who built St. Peter's Square!) It shows four major rivers: Nile I Ganges I Danube I Rio della Plata
They symbolize the four continents that were known at that time:
Africa I Asia I Europe I America

Do you know which river belongs to which continent?
Walk around the fountain, and help Leonardo find the river for each continent!

And what is in the center of the fountain?

- A lion
- Spiderman
- An obelisk

Answer: An obelisk

The Pantheon: temple of all the gods

What does the word *pantheon* mean? It's Greek for "all the gods" (*pan*="all," *theon*="of the gods").

The Pantheon is a huge temple dedicated to all the Roman gods. It is the best-preserved monument in Rome! Emperor Hadrian had it built during the Roman Empire. But since 609 AD, it has been a Catholic church — the Basilica of St. Mary and the Martyrs.

Look up when you stand outside the Pantheon.

The triangle above the entrance is called a "pediment." It has a large sign. Leonardo tried to copy the words, but he missed a few letters. Can you help him complete the words?

M·A_RIP_A·L·F·_OS·TE_TI_M·FE_I_

What does it say? It means "Marcus Agrippa, son of Lucius, consul for the third time, built this." The sign remembers Marcus Agrippa, who created the first Pantheon in 27 BC. It was destroyed by a fire.

Answer: M·AGRIPPA·L·F·COS·TERTIVM·FECIT

Help Leonardo describe the Pantheon by filling in the missing numbers: The entrance of the Pantheon is supported by ________ rows of enormous columns and giant bronze gates. **The first row has ________ columns and the other rows have ________ columns each.**

Answers:
- Three rows
- First row has eight columns
- The other rows have four columns each

Did you know?

The Pantheon's amazing dome is as high as it is wide. It is 43 meters (142 feet) from the floor to the top, and from one side to the other. It's the biggest unsupported concrete dome in the entire world!

Inside the Pantheon —

look up and see the sky!

The real wonder is its breathtaking dome!!
At the top of the dome, there is a hole — called the "oculus." It's open to the sky, and it lets light inside.

The oculus was never covered, so rain falls inside! But they had a smart idea! They built the floor to curve downward. That way, the rainwater could run off into small drains at the edges.

The huge space inside the dome is decorated with ancient sculptures and masterpieces by different artists.

Did you know?
The Pantheon is still used for weddings. And masses are celebrated there on important Catholic holy days.

Near the Pantheon, in the middle of the square, there is a fountain with an Egyptian obelisk. The obelisk was built by Pharaoh Ramses II. It was brought to Italy from the Temple of Ra in the Egyptian city of Heliopolis. Can you guess what style this fountain was built in? Think about the Trevi Fountain and Piazza Navona ...

The SPANISH STEPS ... are you ready to start counting?

Welcome to the **Spanish Steps**, or as the Italians call it, ***Piazza di Spagna***! It's the place where many Italians and tourists from all over the world come to meet each other!

This beautiful square is famous for **... its steps!**

You don't have to count them ... But Leonardo has counted all the steps to be sure of the right number. Guess how many?

A-40 steps   B-85 steps   C-135 steps   D-250 steps

Answer: C-135 stairs

Fill in the missing words:

The stairs connect the ____________________ (Square of Spagna) with ____________________, a baroque church.

Answers: Piazza di Spagna with Trinita dei Monti

Quizzes!

Why do you think it is called the Piazza di Spagna?

A - **Because** the Spanish people paid for this square

B - **Because** the Spanish Embassy is near Vatican City

C - **Because** a Spanish artist built the stairs

At the lower end of the stairs, you can find the Fountain of the Old Boat (or *Fontana della Barcaccia* in Italian). One legend says that after a huge flood of the Tiber River, a little boat was left on this exact spot! That was the inspiration for the fountain's statue!

Answer: B- Because the Spanish Embassy is near Vatican City

Take a break at BioParco Zoo!

Do you want to take a break from seeing monuments, museums, and churches? Leonardo suggests visiting the BioParco Zoo!

Why?

This special zoo has more than 1,000 animals. There are 200 different species of mammals, birds, and reptiles. And most of the animals are in danger of becoming extinct. The BioParco Zoo tries to help the ones that are most at risk.

Follow the signposts located in the zoo! They show you how to find the animals you are looking for ... Be sure to see the King of the Jungle, the lion!

You can also have a lot of fun at the recreation center: the Casina di Raffaello. Here you can find a wooden village, musical instruments, animal farm sculptures ... and so many other things to test your creativity!

Which animals did you see in the zoo?

____

Did you see any special animals that you've never seen before?

____

What is your favorite animal that lives in the BioParco Zoo?

____

Family vote: What was the most impressive thing you saw in the zoo?

____

Explora Museum: learning by doing!

Another good place to take a break – **the Explora Museum!**

This interactive museum was designed for kids. You can explore and learn in many different and fun ways. So let's go ... What do you prefer to be today?

- A scientist
- An astronaut
- A firefighter
- A TV news anchor
- Or ____________

The museum has four areas:

- people
- communication
- environment
- society

Did you know?
Explora is the first museum in Italy created especially for kids! You can explore ecosystems, strange and interesting technology, and much more!

There are many fun rooms where you can play and learn. You can try being a doctor, a physicist, a scientist, a musician ... What areas did you visit? Write them here:

____

Write about what you did:

____

____

Summary of the trip

We had great fun! What a pity it is over ....

How long did you stay in Rome?

____

Where did you stay?

____

What kinds of transportation did you use?

____

Which places did you visit?

____

____

____

What was each family member's favorite place?

__________ : __________

__________ : __________

__________ : __________

__________ : __________

Our family's most favorite place in Rome is:

____

The souvenirs we bought in Rome were:

____

The best food we ate in Rome was:

____

Time for trivia!

Choose the right answer to the questions ...

1. Who was Julius Caesar?

a. A Pope
b. An artist
c. A famous leader of ancient Rome

2. According to a legend, who founded the city of Rome?

a. A gladiator
b. Romulus and Remus
c. A wolf

3. People living in ancient Rome spoke this language:

a. English
b. Italian
c. Latin

4. What is a temple? A place where ...

a. People play football
b. Gods are honored with worship and prayers
c. Animals can graze

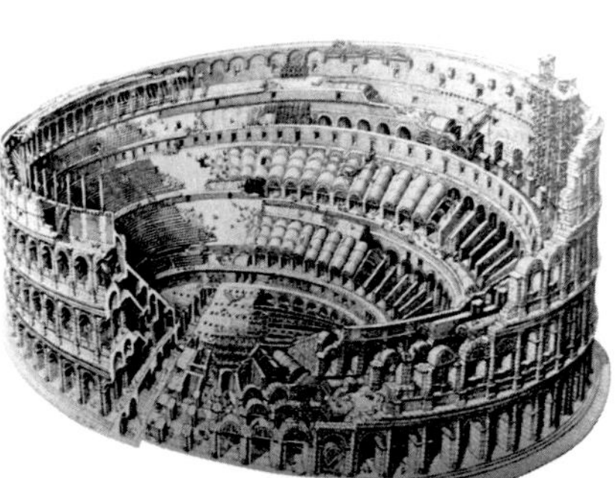

5. What is the Colosseum?

a. A huge, ancient stadium in Rome
b. A modern stadium for playing football
c. A big column in the center of Rome

6. Where does the Pope live today?

a. In a museum
b. In Vatican City
c. In the Sistine Chapel

7. These letters mean the number "8" in Latin: VIII

a. True
b. False

Trivia Answers:
1 - c; 2 - b; 3 - c; 4 - b; 5 - a; 6 - b; 7 - a

8. **What is the best-preserved monument in Rome?**
   a. The Pantheon
   b. The BioParco Zoo
   c. The Spanish Steps

9. **Rome is the capital of Italy?**
   a. True
   b. False

10. **How many years did the Roman Empire last?**
   a. About 100 years
   b. About 20 years
   c. More than 400 years

11. **Who were the gladiators?**
   a. Slaves forced to fight in stadiums like the Colosseum
   b. The most courageous Roman soldiers
   c. The Kings of Rome

12. **Rome is built on four hills.**
   a. True
   b. False

13. **An ingredient in pizza is:**
   a. Grapes
   b. Plain flour
   c. Tortillas

14. **How many rivers cross Rome?**
   a. 5
   b. 1
   c. None

Trivia Answers:
8 - a; 9 - a; 10 - c; 11 - a; 12 - b; 13 - b; 14 - b

A journal

Which places did we visit?

What did we do?

A journal

Which places did we visit?	What did we do?

A journal

Which places did we visit?	What did we do?

Made in the USA
Middletown, DE
14 July 2015